Canvas Mind

It thinks. It feels. It sings.

Dr Preet Agrawal

BookLeaf Publishing

India | USA | UK

Dedication

To my parents, without whom
my mind would be a thoughtless machine.
To my brother, the greatest gift of all time.
To love, given and received in all its forms.
To my deepened respect for art
in its many expressions of beauty.

Preface

My earliest poetry was nothing more than words that needed to escape my mind. Only recently did I begin shaping my thoughts and ideas into this form, one that now feels natural. Each poem in this collection is rooted in real experiences, deeply held beliefs, or emotions genuinely felt.

Most of these pieces were written during the gruelling, sleep-deprived days of medical residency, woven into the fabric of life's trials and transitions. Though born from an exhausted soul, I believe they also reflect the beauty that labor can yield, the way struggle, in its own way, can give rise to something meaningful.

Acknowledgements

I am deeply grateful to my mother for her unwavering belief in me, to my father for his steadfast support, and to my brother for his constant encouragement. Their presence has been a pillar of strength throughout this journey.

I also want to thank my friends and those who have shared in my thoughts, whether with encouragement or critique. Every conversation, challenge, and moment of reflection has helped shape this collection.

This book has been influenced by both joy and hardship, by moments of clarity and uncertainty, and by people both close and distant. To those who embraced my words and even to those who dismissed them, you have all, in some way, contributed to this work.

And to every reader who finds meaning within these pages, thank you. Your time and connection to these words are deeply appreciated.

1. The Search

The search for the meaning of life.
The search for one's purpose.
The search for oneself.

Not everyone embarks on this journey.
Not everyone needs to.
Not everyone does.

For some,
It begins with a sense,
A sense of being lost in the wilderness.
For others,
It has always been their world,
A world of adventures from the very start.

Some may seek their maps to meaning
In a book, a religion, or another's story.
Some may find an inner compass,
Guiding them through the turbulent pass.

Perhaps, for some,
A lone journey would feel meaningless.
Perhaps, for others,
A lone journey is exactly what they need.

2. One Step at a Time

Being,
one step at a time.
Overcoming,
one step at a time.
Growing,
one step at a time.
Becoming,
one step at a time.

And then continuing,
one step at a time.
Evolving,
one step at a time.

3. Patient Patience

Wait, for the relative to give their consent.
Wait, for them to bring
the required procedure's content.

Wait, for the patient to stop moving his head.
Wait, for the anesthetic to sink in, to spread.

Wait, for the drug administered to take effect.
Wait, for the saturation to rise to levels we accept.

Wait, for the blood pressure to climb once more.
Wait, for the pulse- faint at first, then sure.

Wait, in silence, in vigilance, in steady breath.
Wait, between uncertainty and life,
between stillness and death.

❖ *One must endure pain*
to truly grasp another's suffering,
One must know love to feel,
to give, to cherish.
One must taste joy
to understand its fleeting sweetness,
And only in sorrow
can one shed the heaviest tears. ❖

4. Unending Love

Oh, the joy of falling for you
for the first time,
Oh, the joy of being in love with you
for an aeon's time,
Oh, the joy of falling for you
one more time,
Oh, the joy of falling for you,
again and again, every time ...

5. Kyun... ki

Kyun hamesha udaas rehne waala,
aaj sabko muskurate dikh gaya?
Kyunki, mann hi mann,
usne kisi ka muskurata chehra yaad kar liya.

Kyun shaant hai woh,
jiski baaton ke saamn koi kabhi bol nahi paata?
Kyunki woh sun raha usse,
jiske saat waqt bhi kabhi chal nahi paata.

Kyun hamesha thaka rehne waala insaan
aaj itna zinda dikh raha?
Kyunki,ab woh peheli baar
kisi ka pyaar aise mehsoos kar raha.

Kyun hai woh, jisse tha duniya ka darr,
ab azaad hokar jee raha?
Kyunki usse mila hai aisa koi,
jo uski usi se mulaqat karwa raha.

Kyun jo peheli baar khush dikha,
ab phir se shaant dikh raha?
Kyunki sabki pyaari baato me
usse kisi ki chuppi ka kaata chubh raha.

Kyun lagti yeh kavita itni adhuri,
yeh aapne humse poochha?
Kyunki, iske aage kya hua,
yeh koi bhi kabhi jaan na saka.

6. A Silent Ripple

So Beautiful

A soul was offered, unshackled and free,
But the offer returned was friendship's decree.
A deep bond, so beautiful.

The mind was chained to think as everyone knew,
Yet it wandered curiously, in awe of something new.
A nurturing will, so beautiful.

Wandering through the deserted forest
with no one to embark,
A soul once lost now lit the desolate path
through the dark.
A guiding light, so beautiful.

The eyes sparkled in the hues of a golden sunset,
For someone loves to teach, even when they are upset.
A radiant sight, so beautiful.

Unknown to each other before this chance encounter,
How does one become so dear, and then even dearer?
A graceful gift, so beautiful.

I know that making this mistake
will leave you desolate,
But know that, towards me,
you will always have an open gate.
An unwavering affection, so beautiful!

7. The Warmth We Need

They say we need eight hugs a day,
Yet some get none and waste away.
Cold and alone, their souls decay,
Deprived of warmth, they fade to gray.

8. Noise

A Timeless Melody

The first time I affectionately held you...
The first strum we intimately shared...
Yes, we were deaf to the noise too,
But nonetheless, we never really cared.

The noise was chaotic, which is true,
But it brought me an innocent calm.
I was the one holding and fretting you,
Yet you had me dancing within your palm.

Whenever the notes left me without a clue,
You were there, gently holding my arm.
Oh, darling, I do so tenderly love you.
You, my beloved, are my timeless charm.

9. Strings and Echoes

A Symphony of Memories

Another case of a broken string,
Another heart's chord left bleeding,
No more notes could now we play,
For the journeys have lead us astray.
Silent are the strings that used to sing,
Restless, my ears, still hearing them ring.

Several scars to tell several stories,
Those of a past's setting glories.
For grooves were engraved upon the fretboard,
From the memories that melodiously echoed.
You complete me, and it is true,
The symphony was for us, for me and you.

❖

Love lingers,
whether in echoes, silence,
or melodies yet to be played.

❖

10. Tracks

They lay parallel, close yet apart,
Destined to never meet from the very start.
Yet they carve a boundless path to follow,
An endless stretch- stared at, blank and hollow.

My eyes set where the earth meets the sky,
Still, no end- neither closure nor goodbye.
I see the golden sun sink between the tracks,
The heart aches to reach it, then journey back.

The rustling sprinkle of showering rain...
I watch it dissolve the world from the windowpane.
The journey mystically lulls me to sleep,
Oh, the magic of rain, the sun, the rainbow,
I happily weep.

11. Dual Tone of Being Alone

Eternal Void vs Ephemeral Visage

The absence of touch, the ruthless winter's cold,
The lost warmth the mesmerizing rain once told.

An empty seat, waiting eternally for embrace,
A spot once filled with affection's grace.

The desperate plea for a passing voice,
A longing to walk again, if given the choice.

Sadness and sorrow, life a lifeless lie,
Alone with a memory, one smiles to cry.

The feeling of being bound by chains of hollow,
The love that reverberated, leaving its echo.

The former, a curse, the weight of loneliness,
The latter, missing someone, adrift in time and space.

12. Hope

For Vernal Metamorphosis of Frosty Abyss

The moments were filled with joy,
Tickling one's stomach with fluttering butterflies.
They echoed with gleeful, blessed smiles,
Like thunderclaps splitting the heavenly skies.

They were gradually woven over time,
Into an intricate web of memories,
Which froze, broke, vanished in cold,
Devastating, like the originless, unsolved mysteries.

Perhaps this cold is a sign
for the need to move on.
For maybe, despite the unending devotion,
The destination could be long gone.

Lost, directionless, searching for a path,
Yearning solace, one photon might bring,
Infinite toil might someday shed light
From harsh winter to tender spring.

Blindingly dark abyss at absolute zero,
The sheer cold's almighty maximum boom,

Praying to see a crimson flower,
in its tender, loving full bloom.

The loneliness creeps throughout the canvas, Vast sacred
landscape of motionless night.
Maybe the hope keeps someone alive
For coming spring's warmth and sunlight.

13. BANSHEE

Dark, desolate path,
whose was the unhinged scream?
The adventure began,
there was no hidden scheme.
But something happened,
halted for folly in extreme.
It, hopefully praying,
was just a groggy dream.

It was bleak,
seeming, no chance to redeem.
Then lost, adrift,
left in the thoughts' stream.
Scattered thought rays,
they band and they beam.
Waking, it dawned,
it was my own scream.

I was the banshee.

14. Where Darkness Looms

You lie with a breath unsure,
a weak struggle, beautifully pure.
I stay up, watching by your side,
as you fight against the turning tide.

Days and nights blur into weeks,
monitors trace the life they seek.
Harsh lights glare, sleepless and bright,
while restless beeps cut through the night.

Jagged lines waver, rise, then sway,
will you return or drift away?
Fatigue creeps as time moves slow,
but steady hands refuse to let go.

Through darkest hours and breaking dawn,
we fight together, we hold on.
I know it is heavy, I know it is long,
but do not give up. You are strong.

❖

Without searching,
my eyes find you,
A lone candle
in a star-lit sky.

❖

15. Rested

After I rested my mind,
I realised how tired my body was.
After I rested my body,
I realised how tired my mind was.
After I rested them both,
I realised how tired my spirit was.
After I rested my spirit,
I realised how tired my soul was.

16. You Deserve

You deserve another chance,
no matter who slammed the door.
You deserve hands to hold,
even if yours have only known the weight of solitude.
You deserve love,
even if your heart has been an empty house where no
one knocks.
You deserve time to heal,
even if you have only learned to stitch yourself back
together.
You deserve to let go,
even if the past still lingers like an echo in your bones.
You deserve the ocean,
even if you have spent a lifetime swallowing dust,
if the only salt you have known is from your wounds.

And when no one says it, when silence answers back,
you still do.

17. Make or Break

No one is coming to save you.
No one will press their hands
to your wounds to call it love.
No one will knock on the door
of an empty house to light a fire inside.

You are not owed time to heal.
The past will not release you.
You either let go
or you carry it until your spine breaks.

You were born choking on dust.
You can either swallow it or you can spit.

And when silence answers back,
make it wish it hadn't.

18. Where the Spirit Flows

The words from the soul of a writer
Were gibberish to a foreign mind,
Ink spilled its truth in nurtured lines,
Yet lost to minds in cages confined.

The dancer, like waves in tranquil water,
Gliding on mist through morning air,
Grace unfolding, light as a whisper,
Yet met with silence, stiff and bare.

The hum from the heart of a singer
Was noise to the tone-deaf ear,
A melody woven through the air,
Unheard by those unwilling to hear.

The painter bled colors on canvas,
Trapping sunrise in liquid gold,
To eyes that knew only shades of gray,
It was nothing, dull and cold.

Expression takes form in motion and sound,
In colors and words where meaning is found.

Art speaks, it moves, it sings, it glows,
But only where the spirit flows.

25

19. An Everlasting Moment

Today, yet again,
I see myself in a familiar place,
Recalling the night's allure
in its serene and elegant embrace.

That moment was exhilarating,
thanks to its calm, fiery beauty,
Knowing it was always fleeting,
filled me with deep humility.

Though long gone,
it lingers in my mind, ever bolder;
Realizing again,
beauty lies in the eye of the beholder.

Its fleeting nature adds to its beauty,
elevating it above,
While our choice to immortalize it
fills it with love.

❖

Healing is neither fast nor linear;
it arrives like waves,
carrying us forward with time.

❖

20. Unburdened

To stand unshaken in my own skin,
woven in comfort, soft and thin.
To speak with fire, never fearing,
echoing out loud, unwavering, hearing.

To walk with ease, no measured pace,
no watchful eyes, no rigid grace.
Each step its own, unchained, untamed,
a journey walked, yet unashamed.

To shed the weight of past disguise,
no need for masks, no fear of eyes.
To carve a truth in stone and air,
and never flinch beneath a stare.

To rise when storms would bid one break,
to bend yet never quite forsake.
To meet the winds with steady breath,
undaunted by their whispered death.

To roam unbound, as all should be,
yet knowing freedom is not so free.
It favors some heavily, while others pay,
a light for some, a shadowed day.

21. Panning Out, Unorchestrated

It did not come with fanfare bright,
nor in the season I had planned.
No script was set, no fate in sight,
no careful placing, hand in hand.

Yet still it came, a quiet thing,
not less for missing a perfect cue.
Not every bird must greet the spring
to make its song more pure, more true.

We chase the paths both straight and kind,
a story that bends to what we crave.
But beauty laughs at a plan designed,
unfolding where it means to wave.

So let it come, though late, though strange,
not less in worth, not dim in hue.
For even when the stars rearrange,
the sky above is just as blue.

www.ingramcontent.com/pod-product-compliance
Lightning Source LLC
Chambersburg PA
CBHW071237140726
47996CB00007B/2646